MY FIRST BOOK
MEXICO

ALL ABOUT MEXICO FOR KIDS

GLOBED
CHILDREN BOOKS

Copyright 2023 by Globed Children Books

All rights reserved. No part of this book may be reproduced or distributed in any form without prior written permission from the author, with the exception of non-commercial uses permitted by copyright law.

Limited of Liability/Disclaimer of Warranty: The publisher and author make no representations or liabilities with respect to the accuracy and completeness of the contents of this work and specifically disclaim all warranties including without limitations warranties of fitness of particular purpose. No warranty may be created or extended by sales or promotional materials. This work is sold with the understanding that the publisher and author is not engaging in rendering medical, legal or any other professional advice or service. Further, readers should be aware that websites listed in this work may have changed or disappeared between when this work was written and when it is read.

Interior and cover Design: Daniel Day
Editor: Margaret Bam

For My Sons, Daniel, David and Jude

Izamal, Yucatan, Mexico

Mexico

Mexico is a **country**.

A country is land that is controlled by a **single government**. Countries are also called **nations, states, or nation-states**.

Countries can be **different sizes**. Some countries are big and others are small.

Morelia Michoacan, Mexico

Where Is Mexico?

Mexico is located in the continent of **America.**

A continent is **a massive area of land that is separated from others by water or other natural features**.

Mexico is situated in the **northern part of America.**

Traditional Mexican houses in Mexico City, Mexico

Capital

The capital city of Mexico is Mexico City.

Mexico City is located in the **central part** of the country.

Mexico City is the largest city in Mexico.

Cabo San Lucas, Mexico

States

Mexico is divided into 31 states and one federal district, which is the capital, Mexico City.

The states of Mexico are

Aguascalientes, Baja California, Baja California Sur, Campeche, Chiapas, Chihuahua, Coahuila, Colima, Durango, Guanajuato, Guerrero, Hidalgo, Jalisco, México (State of Mexico), Michoacán, Morelos, Nayarit, Nuevo León, Oaxaca, Puebla, Querétaro, Quintana Roo, San Luis Potosí, Sinaloa, Sonora, Tabasco, Tamaulipas, Tlaxcala, Veracruz, Yucatán, and Zacatecas.

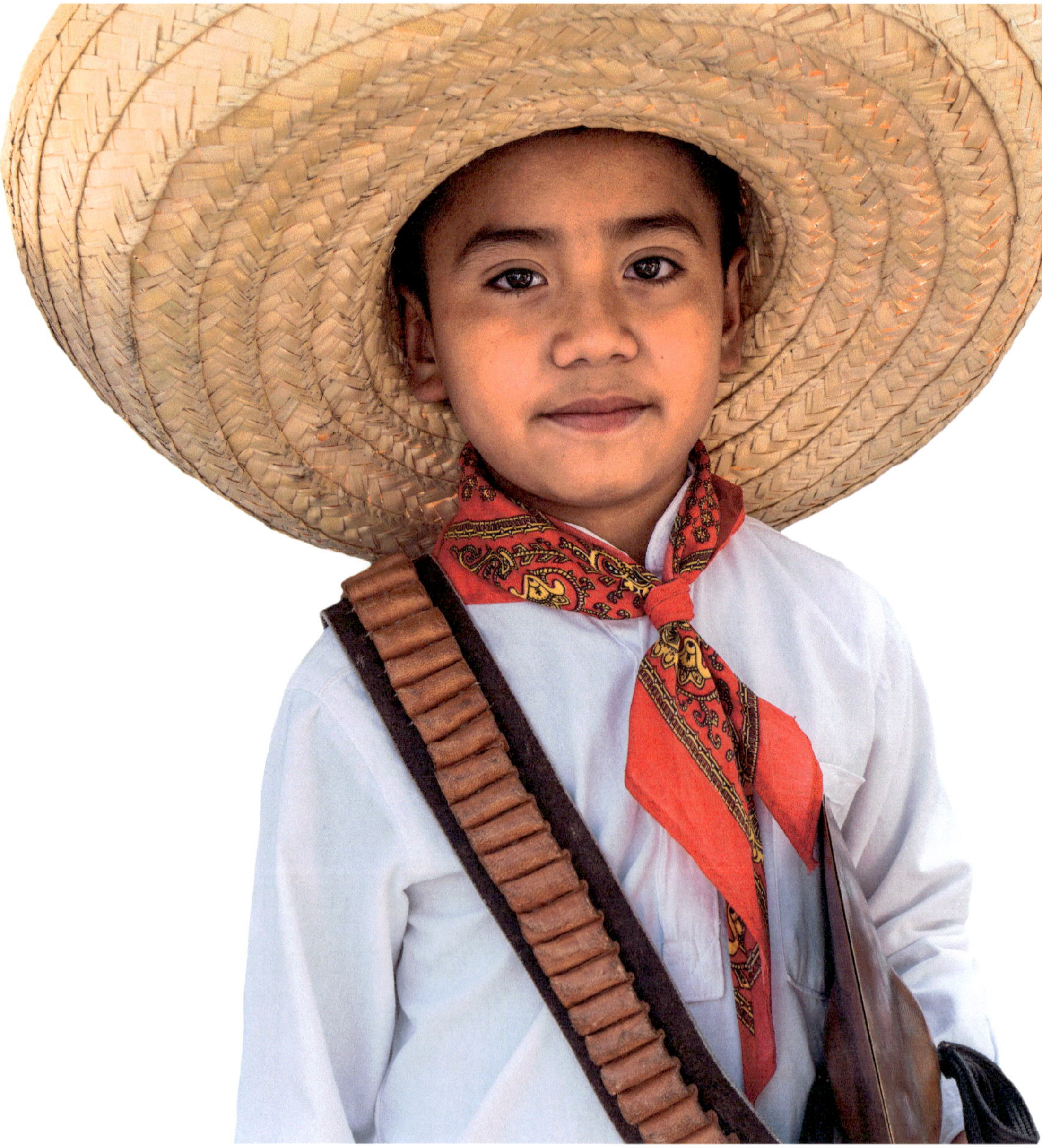

Population

Mexico has a population of around **128 million people** making it the 11th most populated country in the world.

Puerto Vallarta, Mexico

Size

Mexico is **1,972,550 square kilometres** making it the 13th largest country in the world by area.

Mexico is known for its diverse geography, which includes deserts, tropical forests, mountains, and coastal plains.

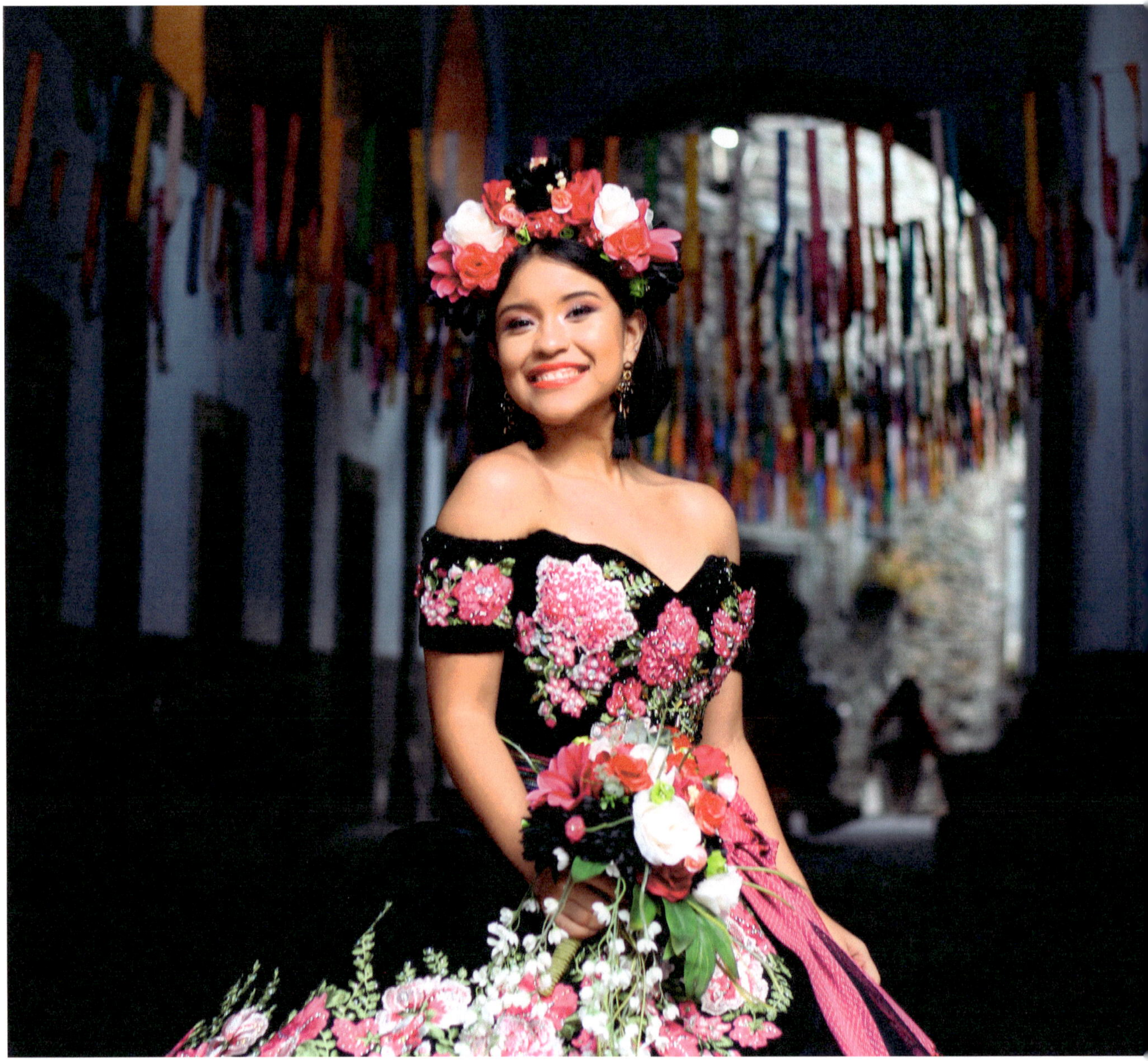

Languages

The national language of Mexico is **Spanish.** Spanish is the fourth most spoken language in the world after Mandarin Chinese, English, and Hindi.

Here are a few phrases and sayings in Spanish
- **Hola: Hello**
- **Buenas: Hi (informal)**
- **Buenas noches: Good evening**
- **Bienvenido: Welcome**
- **Buenas noches: Good night**
- **Que te vaya bien: Have a good day**

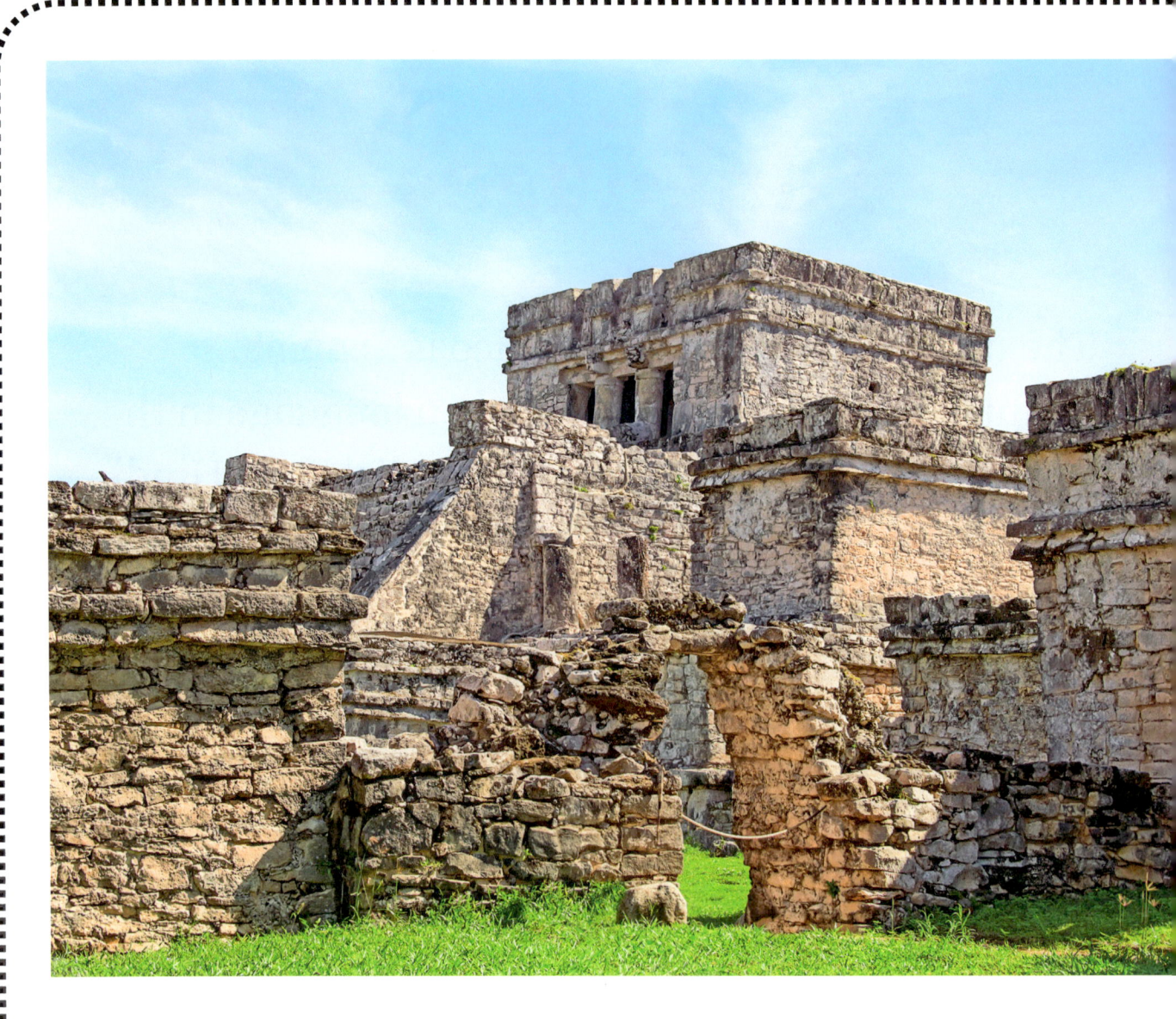

Ruins of the Mayan Fortress and temple, Tulum, Mexico

Attractions

There are lots of interesting places to see in Mexico.

Some beautiful places to visit in Mexico are

- Xcaret
- Museo Nacional de Antropologia
- Chichen Itza
- Tulum Archaeological Site
- Rio Secreto
- Chapultepec Castle

Palenque in Chiapas, Mexico

History of Mexico

Mexico has a long and fascinating history that dates back thousands of years. The region was inhabited by various indigenous peoples for thousands of years before the arrival of the Spanish in the 16th century.

The Spanish colonized Mexico and established a colonial government, which lasted for over 300 years.

In the early 19th century, Mexico gained independence from Spain and established a republic.

Dia de los Muertos

Customs in Mexico

Mexico has many fascinating customs and traditions.

- **Quinceañera is a traditional Mexican celebration that marks a girl's 15th birthday and her transition from childhood to adulthood.**
- **Day of the Virgin of Guadalupe is religious holiday celebrated in Mexico on December 12th, which honours the Virgin Mary and includes processions, parades, and other celebrations.**
- **Dia de los Muertos is a traditional Mexican holiday celebrated on November 1st and 2nd honouring deceased loved ones.**

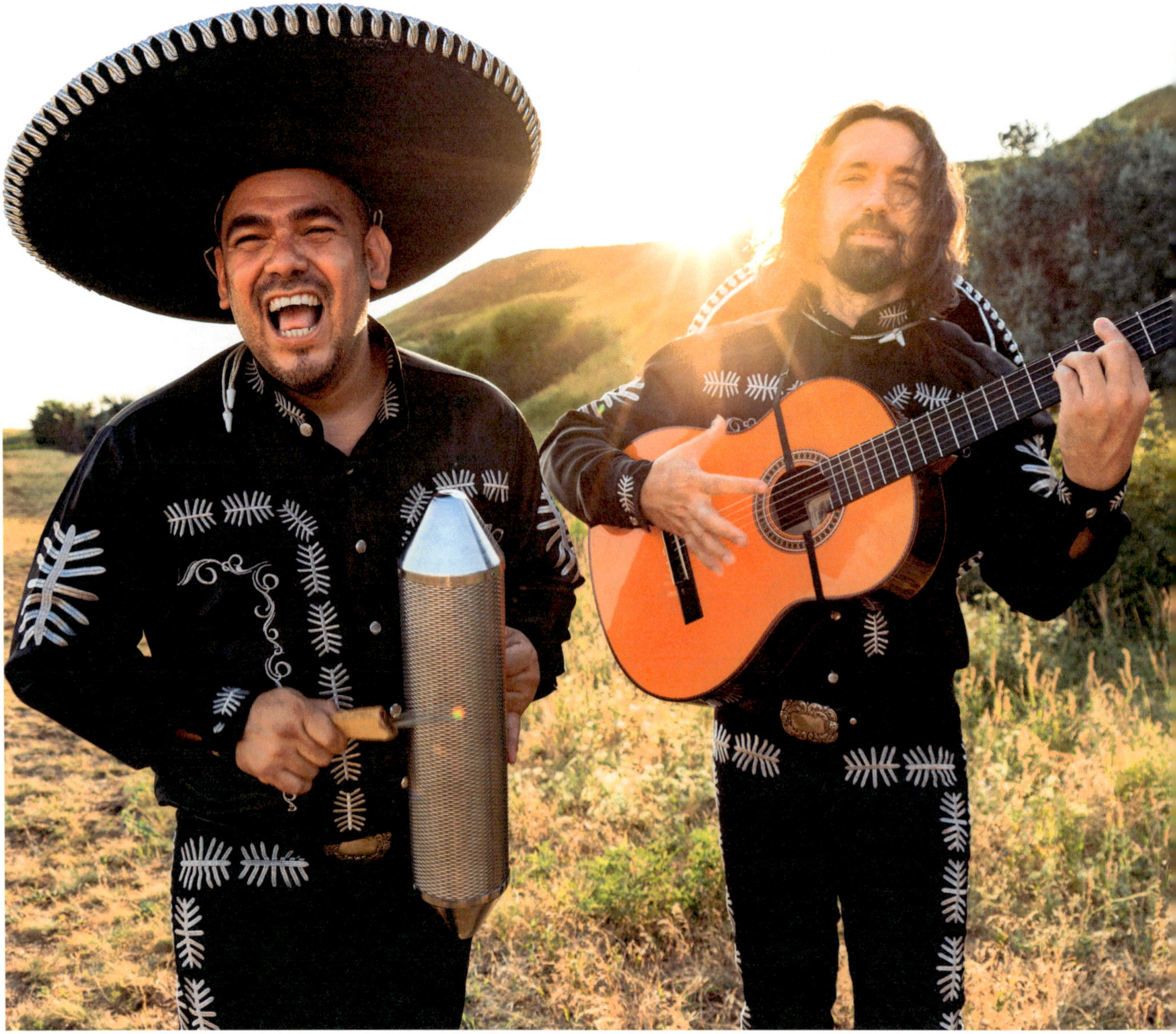

Music of Mexico

There are many different music genres in Mexico such as such as **Ranchera, Banda, Norteño and Mariachi.**

Some notable Mexican musicians include
- **Juan Gabriel - Singer and songwriter known for his romantic ballads and mariachi music.**
- **Vicente Fernández - Singer known for his ranchera music and iconic mustache.**
- **Selena - Singer known for her Tejano music and influential impact on Mexican-American culture.**

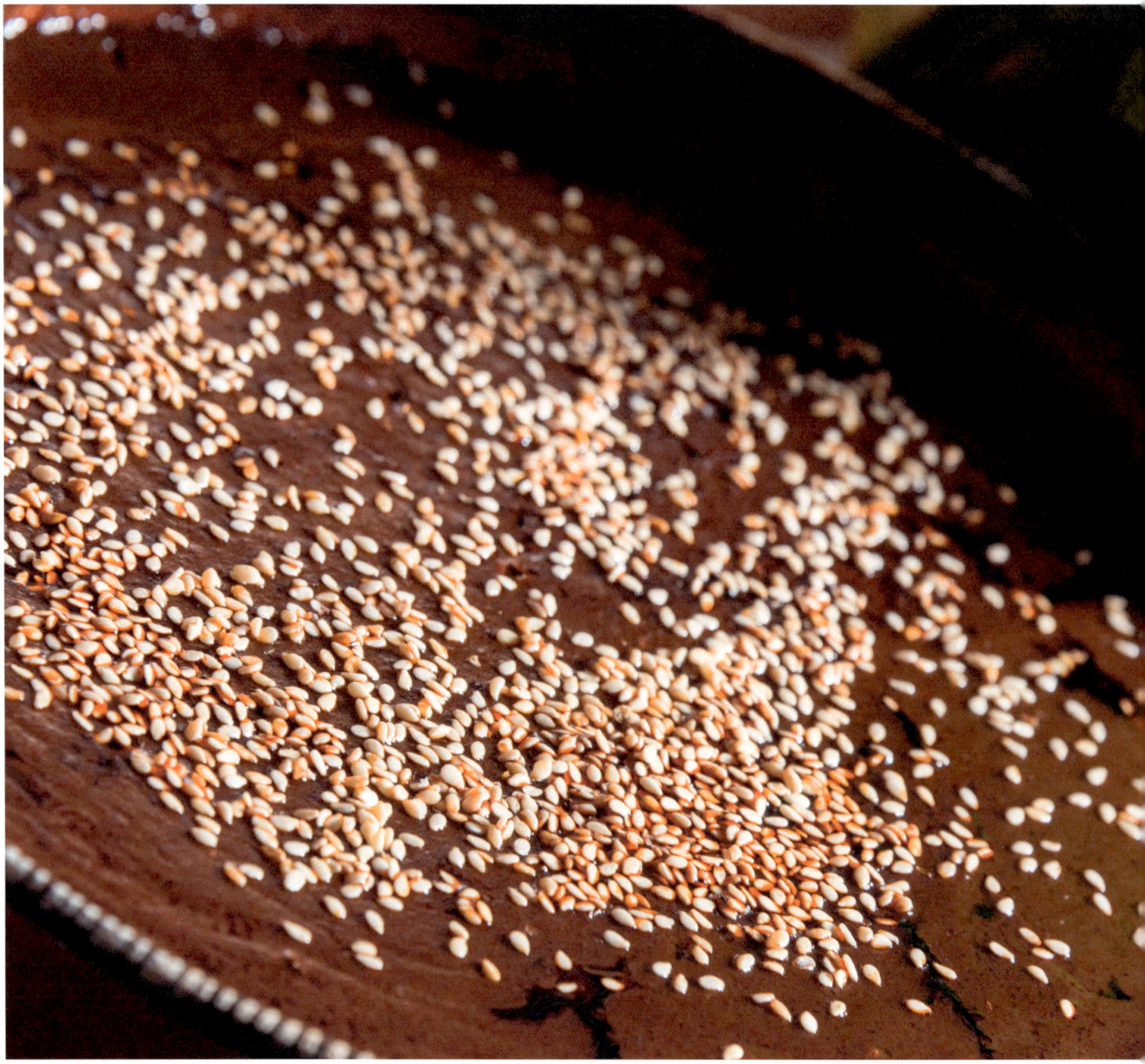

Food of Mexico

Mexican food is known for being tasty, delicious and flavoursome.

The national dish of Mexico is **Mole** which is a delicious sauce made with hot chiles, rich chocolate, spices, and tomatillos.

Tacos

Food of Mexico

Mexican cuisine is diverse and flavourful, with a focus on fresh, locally sourced ingredients.

Some popular dishes in Mexico include

- **Tacos** - Soft or hard tortillas filled with various meats, vegetables, and spices.
- **Enchiladas** - Tortillas stuffed with meat or beans, rolled up, and covered with a spicy tomato or chili sauce.
- **Pozole** - A traditional soup made with hominy, meat, and a spicy broth, topped with cabbage, radishes, and lime juice.

Xochimilco, Mexico City, Mexico

Weather in Mexico

Mexico is large country with a range of climates, from tropical to desert and mountainous regions.

The coastal regions have a tropical climate with high temperatures and humidity, while the central plateau has a temperate climate with cooler temperatures. The northern regions are arid and have hot summers and mild winters, while the southern regions have a more humid, tropical climate.

Mexican wolf

Animals of Mexico

There are many wonderful animals in Mexico.

Here are some animals that live in Mexico

- Mexican wolf
- Jaguar
- Axolotl
- Spider monkeys
- Ocelot
- Coati

Playa Del Norte, Isla Mujeres, Mexico

Beaches

There are many beautiful beaches in Mexico which is one of the reasons why so many people visit this beautiful country every year.

Here are some of Mexico's beaches

- **Playa Norte · Isla Mujeres**
- **Playa La Ropa · Zihuatanejo, Mexico**
- **Balandra Beach · La Paz, Mexico**
- **Playa El Cielo · Cozumel. Mexico**

Football with Mexico flag

Sports in Mexico

Sports play an integral part in Mexican culture. The most popular sport is **Football.**

Here are some of famous sportspeople from Mexico

- **Hugo Sánchez - Soccer**
- **Rafael Márquez - Soccer**
- **Fernando Valenzuela - Baseball**
- **Lorena Ochoa - Golf**
- **Julio César Chávez - Boxing**
- **Saúl "Canelo" Álvarez - Boxing**

Frida Kahlo

Famous

Many successful people hail from Mexico.

Here are some notable Mexican figures

- **Frida Kahlo - Artist**
- **Diego Rivera - Artist**
- **Carlos Slim Helu - Businessman**
- **Salma Hayek - Actress**
- **Guillermo del Toro - Filmmaker**
- **Octavio Paz - Poet and Essayist**

Morelia Michoacan, Mexico

Something Extra...

As a little something extra, we are going to share some lesser known facts about Mexico

- **Mexico is home to the world's smallest volcano named the Cuexcomate, which is only 43 feet tall.**
- **Mexico is the birthplace of many popular foods, such as tacos, and guacamole.**

Uxmal, Mexico

Words From the Author

We hope that you enjoyed learning about the wonderful country of Mexico.

Mexico is a country rich in culture and beauty, with lots of wonderful places to visit and people to meet.

We hope you continue to learn more about this wonderful nation. If you enjoyed this book, consider leaving a review!

With Love

Made in United States
Troutdale, OR
04/19/2025